Arctic Journal

Arctic Journal

STEPHEN PAX LEONARD

THE CHOIR PRESS

First published in the United Kingdom in 2014 by
The Choir Press

ISBN 978-1-909300-62-0

For my Grandfather, *In Memoriam*

Note

This poem was written during the year of 2010-2011, much of it during the dark period when there is no sun at all for three and a half months in north-west Greenland. I lived amongst the Inugguit or Polar Eskimos who live in the northern most permanently inhabited settlement in the world, documenting the language and oral traditions of a society of Inuit hunters numbering 700. Living alone in three different remote Inuit settlements for a year (without leaving the region), the *Arctic Journal* is a response to the transient Arctic landscape, the transcendental voices of the hunters blurring the poet's insider/outsider distinction, the intimacy of the enmeshed natural and human environment, the vicissitudes of life in the polar desert, the liberty of thought that the open spaces of the North offers, the awakening of primordial intuitions, the isolation and solitude, but also the troubling human environment seen through a very subjective lens. The sense of self that one discovers in the remote polar night, the various colours and sounds of community and wilderness would lead me to conjugate and juxtapose words and images in new and novel ways. The blurred soundscape would reverberate through my mind and out in the white desert I was exposed in a unique way to the possibilities of poetry in the begetting and forgetting of cold days. *Arctic Journal* is the result of those personal thoughts and ethnographic encounters over a period of twelve months. It is based on the chronology of my year in the Arctic and I have thus called it *Arctic Journal*.

But the poem is more than my reflections on an alluring Arctic landscape and Inuit social life, it is also in part a semi-didactic criticism of contemporary issues such as globalisation, climate change, the decline of the nation and the race to the bottom in standards, decency and conduct in modern Britain. It is a privileged perspective on a rapidly changing world seen by a disillusioned romantic standing at the very top of it.

SPL

February, 2014

Acknowledgements

I would like to thank the Master and Fellows of Trinity Hall, Cambridge for allowing me to intermit my Fellowship and undertake my research in the Polar North. Back in Cambridge, Trinity Hall provided me with the perfect home to write up my field notes, produce academic publications as well as a stimulating environment for completing *Arctic Journal*.

I

Pytheas and Polybius manufactured the ancient myth,

The palindromic place-name only came later,

Qaanaaq, a place of tangled ken and kith,

Now, a US Air Base bears the *onoma*,

Thule, a polar desert at the top of the world,

Moss, lichen, permafrost, never-ending light,

Rocks, boulders and scree, *imprimis*,

Deceptive distances, Arctic clarity, bright

Barren tundra, unfenced wilderness,

With meteoritic coastlines that mirror the moon

Whale-shaped Herbert Island is within my grasp,

This baleen of rock, awash in crimson,

Pantone, crayola, peach and persimmon,

Late summer, scumbled sky,

Blue skies, day-after-day,

These endless, halcyon days of August,

Whose panoply of light may

Offer a reprieve from choked cities, smog-hidden polities

The laughing Raven banks down,

Joking at the frenzied sledge dogs

Whose shouts and cheers echo around the place,

Racked by hunger and in a sorry state,

They bid farewell to the Royal Arctic Line,

Whose blood-red hull melts, sublime,

In the evening butter-gold sky,

Her rotating futtocks and then she heads south,

Gone my dear, for another year

2

Lonely cathedrals of ice, turning blue, sit like moored ships,
Their west-looking escutcheons, amphitheatres of light,
Hungry glacial tongues lick the opposite shore,
Tufty-headed cotton grass sways in the breeze,
Arctic Poppies galore, yellow flowers, hairy stems,
And Snow Buntings chatter and chirp cheerily,
Oblivious to towers of ice crashing into the sea,
Like controlled explosions,
Scattering ice like confused debris,
A colony of Arctic Terns, black napes and white cheeks,
Escort a pod of bulbous Belugas,
Out of the bay, beyond and beyond

The *Monodon monoceros* or unicorn of the sea,
The laborious toil and elusive spoils of the Inugguit,
Estivates in local waters, gestates in still quarters,
Precarious pods in the fjord, hunted with harpoons,
From a silent kayak with an at-the-ready *avataq*,[1]
Formed by a cruel woman dragged into the ocean,
Whose long hair twisted into a pointed lance,
The frozen product of folklore and myth,
And a herd of walrus is said to be close,
Throat-singers huff and puff, mimicking the bull's call,
Whistling and grunting, sliding and shunting
Into sidings for the night, into sunken ridings out of sight

4

II

Peary, Rasmussen, Cook, to name but a few,

Explorers whose tatty photos,

Hang above the corner pew,

Souvenirs of another era, memories that some rue,

Their progeny live on, but the pride is gone,

Symbols of the *kadluna* par excellence,[2]

Whose reckless ambition to conquer nature,

Made them the enemy and the traitor,

Whose desire to be Number 1 at any cost,

Meant that the Inugguit who took them there,

Felt forgotten and lost

Inugguit chimneys light up toothless grins in the mist,

Vaporised words linger in arid self-interrogation,

Whose syllables lurch like a ship starting to list,

In rough waters of words that wallow towards port.

Hunters whisper implausible palindromes over black coffee,

During the interstices of everyday life,

Bemused silences and then a sesquipedalian,

The conversation palls and then,

Drunkenness shouts from a window,

Disfigured grins gesture me in,

To join the din,

To join the festival of glazed, almond eyes,

Alcohol running insidiously through the veins,

These feckless few seek solace in new pastimes,

For which they lack the right enzyme,

Pleated wrinkles smile back at me, sardonically,

This ethereal daze, these endless summer days

The *ammaqa* spirit pervades the place,[3]

Maybe, maybe not, but don't lose face,

No pledge, covenant or word is my bond,

Clocks, appointments and diaries are white man's tools,

The accoutrements of Europeans and fools,

Time is told with the seasons, sea ice and the wind,

A life measured out by spoons of sugar,

And stools in yellow bags,

And the morning tractor – chug, chug, chug

The honey wagon – my alarm call,

Suddenly, at the entrance hall,

Hainanghunai, Hainanghunai …[4]

III

Sunday at 10am; a distant peal as reminiscent church bells toll,
A bronchial stand-in catechist stumbles over polysyllabic words,
A Decalogue of sin is read in a staccato,
Muttering monotone, a stuttering microphone,
A chorus of coughing in the back pews,
Shuffling and snorting, whispering and cavorting,
Tubercular disinterest and disengagement,
The solemn, sober Congregation
Leaves silently, remembering *Kuuti*[5]
And making sure their religion is a matter
Between God and them, *only*

The sky is a see-saw tipping west,
Sinking the sun and rising the moon,
At the day's bequest,
Tilted-eyed *qimmit* bay the rising gibbous,[6]
In an eerie concert of evening solitude,
Whose sublime symphony is my nocturnal melody
Whose painful litany is my nightly threnody.
The *isblomster* that border the window pane,
Complex, variegated October vignettes,
The concertinaed folds of the granite accordion in the East,
Radiated hues of red and purple in late summer,
Until late August at least,
But now, uncompromisingly white,
The Snow Buntings gathered and have gone,
The harbinger of winter,
Now, there is no twitter

Leviathan ice cubes accumulate on the desert, transcendental shore

In a paradoxical otherworldliness, surreal and without clocks,

Disturbed sleep summons succubus,

And the sound of snow-caked boots on the step,

On September nights with falling mercury,

That used to freeze, *qanga hiur'du*,[7]

Like sleeping in the bleachers,

The warble of the oil heater is my company,

Garrulous wind, chatting down the chimney,

The hut trembles in the northern stiff wind,

Florid complexions through the *fenestra*,

A studied silence and then another non-sequitur

Bosky Bingo for the inveterate gamblers and *taffimut* it is,[8]

Lively Polka, whaling songs and slurs,

Smiles and the accordionist descants and jigs,

A bevy of boisterous Eskimos stagger and tumble,

On display, the limits of bodily abandon,

Mumbo-jumbo,

Ladies' faces marred with tears,

Inebriated, schizophrenic Friday nights,

That end in accusations and forgotten fights,

Fixed, expressionless looks and clenched jaws that do not lie,

Snared by their blitheness,

Their quarry is the visitor from afar,

Well-oiled xenophobes' horizons stretch not far,

Osculated are those that leave, the last to deceive

Cerulean icebergs parked on a beach of snow,

Their chatoyant bellies shimmering glaucously,

Bored sledge dogs stand sentry for another summer,

A dead Harp Seal on the shore below,

All blood-stained and wishbone shaped markings,

The dogs are asleep, curled up, tight balls of fur,

Tail over head, oblivious to the circling scuds instead,

An esurient hound spots its feeder from afar,

Forgotten laundry hangs on frosted lines over discarded furniture,

Eskimos shuffle from house to house,

Track-suited, puffing smoke, playing a practical joke,

Pulling in their mist, toddlers on wooden *qamutiks*[9]

During the interstices of everyday life

IV

A gaunt landscape on a bleak afternoon,

Except for the wind, a tossed silence,

A fighting, obstreperous murder of Ravens wheel over the dump,

And the thump, thump of the helicopter overhead,

This grammarless landscape without rules,

Syntax, morphology or Chomskyian tools,

The land and the sky merge to form a patina of subtle blends,

The grey and white of the Kittiwake flying over thin ice,

Candles flicker nervously behind frosted window panes,

The sky lours,

Worried wives wait behind wooden window frames,

In silent rooms without verbiage,

Armed with binoculars, scanning the horizon for lost husbands,

Two views merged into one misty panorama,

Blurred sledges with imposing stanchions jounce over snow-covered scree,

The sun hidden behind a mackerel-coloured façade,

Drum-songs are sung, but there is no bard

An orange wan stain on the horizon,

The soft, diffused light of late October is vague and uncertain,

A crepuscular incoherence,

The twilight of a faded postcard,

Wistful looking dogs, the tenants of the scree slopes,

Watch my gait with quizzical expressions,

Heads rotating slowly, hypnotically,

In the peninsular light,

Dead dogs lie *rigor mortis* in street side morgues,

Shot for having broken from their chains,

Or for lacking the correct social mores,

Heads pulled back to their withers,

Expressions of horror and dried, frozen blood,

Are worn stiffly under a *kafan* of thin, white snow,

A shroudless corpse on a tense, silent track,

A gaunt landscape on a bleak afternoon

Naulaghaqtoq sits like a light bulb[10]

In the western November sky,

Casting her Venusian light over the place,

The gelatinous soup thickens,

Elements scrap over stricken frazil crystals

And *nilas*,

Nothing to be done, just listen to *hila*,[11]

The sea ice creaks and groans,

Tides stymied, moods timid

Pregnant mums preambulate and push,

Prams, around and around

An extended family where reputation determines all,

No muddled genealogies here,

Quidnuncs at Thule run the rumour mill,

Hypochondria, apathy,

Bridled enthusiasm and weekend society ill,

Rankled by criticism, strangled by socialism,

The former Mayor parades his Falstaffian bulk,

Displaced and motivation adrift,

Carefree, unmortgaged lives in a static society,

Questioning orbs on an indifferent place,

Curiosity absent, old traditions spent,

Children are left unchided, sometimes unprovided,

A community built on socialist ideals and gossip,

But materialism is now everywhere,

The world over wants the latest this and that

He who gives quietus to the rumour,

Sprigs skitter across frozen puddles,

Inugguaq, the 'great' or the 'big' man,

Or perhaps, the 'paradoxical' Lilliputian,

Manacled by shyness, but without ambage,

Peals of laughter and practical jokes,

The risible Inugguit who live

In the best of all possible worlds,

Panaglossian, but worn down by tragedy,

All tuned in to the radio,

Waiting for Bingo in stereo,

Honeyed tones, a crackle, and then

The sound of television static,

Tschhhhhhhhhhhhhhh,

Like an erratic Arabian sandstorm,

Scanning, hissing and then mirth on air

On a bleak Monday afternoon

Now the shamans have fallen silent,

The *angakkoq* has flown away,[12]

Or is perhaps just underground,

The Sampo has been stolen,

And all the credos of a former, but recent time

And all the fagged out credenda,

Lost to a keen wind,

But Pentecostalism has been found,

Divine healing, glossolalia and spiritual gifts,

Preaching nonsense to those adrift,

Now, no more *katzenjammer* for the Born-Again,

But, what is the cost of this fundamentalist *Gestalt*?

V

In November, the sea ice is hummocky,

A frozen, checkered collision of rubble,

Many a chilled mickle makes a frigid muckle,

A museum of ice, statues leaning like drunks

On lamp posts with antique glacial trunks,

The hazy, winter moon with her whitish areolas,

Long winter nights, maze of constellations and planets,

But no aurora,

A spangled firmament is my view,

Celestial bliss, too fine to miss,

Shooting stars like planes falling out of the sky,

Crunching snow under foot,

Snowy tracks lit by broad shoulders of streetlights,

Whose noses point down inquisitively, accusingly

Hunters' homes without lampshades or pelmets,

Oriels, gilded edges, gauds, lace trim or nets,

No books on the shelf, no libretto, no Delft,

All at sixes and sevens inside,

Adolescent boys hang from the ceiling, noosed,

Swinging to a premature dirge,

The ultimate scourge,

Singing the end of summer,

Before endless piles of washing-up,

And then, a *qivittoq* on the beach,[13]

And bubbling walrus in stew pots,

Frozen Char melts in the mouth,

Pungent blubber lying on racks,

Narwhal meat unfurled on cardboard plates,

Gibbier hanging from rusty hooks,

Stretched seal skins dry in the breeze

In this place without trees

Glottal stops and breathy, suspiring vowels linger

In chaotic rooms with stories to tell,

This demotic language of sighs and groans,

Which is more than just grammar and monotone,

Fewer than a chiliad strong,

Syllable upon syllable upon syllable and then breathe,

Whistles and whispers like the wind through the vents,

A language without proverbs,

Avani, *hamani*, *pavani* and *pikani*,

And over there, down there, up there,

Way over there and beyond a bit

How can our tongues be so different?

Our interactions so incoherent

Are the limits of my language the limits of my world?

All I know is what I have words for

Wovon man nicht sprechen kann, darüber muss man schweigen

VI

Swaddled in Erebus, my view is monochromatic blackness,

The day has gone and still no sun,

Deprived of light, my head is sore,

Darkness internalised to the core.

Drowsiness weighs upon me,

And the exigencies of solitude,

And the demands of *Manque-du-tout*,

The faculae of the magnificent half moon,

Providing welcome and generous light,

To the shadowy room,

To this Cimmerian, increasingly eternalised darkness,

Which leaves my mind addled and somewhere else,

Eyelids closed for much of the morn,

When will I awake from this lethargic dream?

Or is this a fraudulent scheme?

Qaanaaq, a cluster of cobalt yellow lights huddled together,

Over the brow of a hill, but on the edge,

Down the dark, dank track,

Where curled chimney smoke is fraternal,

Silent television sets light up every room,

Test Card F in cyan, magenta and blue,

Has been playing for some hours now,

The picture tears slightly, horizontally,

Glued to alien images, and not conversation,

Home is the Ministry of Children,

A fairground of fun and freedom,

No dwelling of Doric discipline,

No abode of airy ambition

The first Sunday of Advent,

Shining stars in windows, carols,

Dancing around the Christmas tree,

A Norwegian Spruce sambas in the wind,

A speech, like a solemn prothalamion

Hand in hand, we chaunt,

Around and around, we flaunt

No sunset, no sunrise,

Just the nothingness of the polar darkness,

Intoxicating obscurity,

The dogs' endless cries,

Scoreless Kaaba coloured sky,

Drunk on darkness, winter monochrome,

Hibernal, creeping confusion,

And hanging delirium,

How long is a day in the dark?

At noon, he emerges from his truckle-bed,

To see the tantalising wafer of light,

A promise of future respite,

A transient smidge of unaudited hope,

Peeking through the infinite ether,

Then, celestial curtains close the brief skylight,

Orion is wheeled on at two in the afternoon,

Oneiric nights; at dawn talk of dreams and the moon,

The full moon, and this nocturnal chiaroscuro

VII

Lugubrious December offers time to the pensive one,

In a forgotten corner of the Arctic,

Sequestered at home, in the hut,

Where it is all ship-shape and Bristol fashion,

Trying to winnow the responses and statements

From this alien community,

No dawn, no dusk, the poet lost in sub-fusc,

Has misplaced his mettle amidst his decaying fettle

Misted mirror in refrigerated latrine,

Splayed silence over fuming cha,

A mnemonic landscape turned black,

The toil of darkness is never-ending,

Then, a hiatus in the brumal palinode,

But the poet sits with a headache of darkness,

Cloaked in the beetle black-gown,

Of the now silent Raven,

Like some biblical penitence,

In this wintry adagio

A place in disequilibrium,

Centuries old balance lost to the West,

The Arctic hunters of the Far North,

– a symbol of a rapidly changing world –

A patriarchal society,

Those with the Vice of the Greeks

Best not come forth,

Still, war is a stranger to these people,

Hurhuktut is a word for other lands,[14]

In a world of too many people,

Here, a bungled transition from nomad to sedent,

Such haste, no place for the waste,

Non-biodegradable black bags pile up and up,

Without a thought for future solutions or pollution

Subsistence economy, in patches,

According to his dispatches,

From blithe spirit to welfare dependent victim,

Hunting restrictions ordained from a distant place,

Threaten a way of life, but add to the knowledge base

And the hoary winter has turned mild again,

Scales are tipped and soon turmoil,

Snow in September, rain in December,

A month into winter, thirty degrees warmer than the last,

What is this lunacy?

What are we to believe?

We await the Stygian outcome, the days and the sun

Memory is the hunters' key asset,

Currency and entertainment in a scriptless place,

Knowledge stored in the head,

Passed down orally,

Inherited from ear to ear,

But they say it will disappear.

The Inugguit read the ice with refined ken, not books,

Schooling is on the syllabus, (but not Polybius)

But brings few benefits to the indigenous mind

VIII

The Polar Eskimos are an experiential lot,
Abstraction and negotiation are alien,
If there is no abstract in an empty place,
should we conceive just reality?
He asks politely.
Is a fork a fork if it has no tines?
Is a bell a bell if it has no chime?
Carpe diem is the social imperative,
Live and let live, I am told
Carpe diem, quam minimum credula postero
The present tense is all that counts,
Savers, investors, those who look at future days,
Subjects of suspicion and Inugguit frowns

A cemetery of youth, perched above the sea,
Unrequited love, suicide, rest beneath the scree,
An emotional decree cometh from problem-sharing taboo,
Closed minds in a closed society,
Inferiority complex, anxious not to be the *Untermensch*,
Intellectual curiosity is a foreign, superfluous plea,
Public shame in a tiny place is a price too high to pay,
Pangs of pathos hang from the wall,
Memories of those who were too proud to say all,
Photographs of teenagers lost to an unworthy cause
In the sleepless summers of last year and the year before

Squeezed by a host of factors,

Space closing in around them,

Voices threatening to vanish with the ice,

Drum-songs, storytelling, myths,

No longer suffice,

All inextricably linked to *hiku* and[15]

Replaced by endless television,

Aping and multiplying the ways of the West,

The endless flicker of this visual age,

The mindless violence of the cinematic stage,

Bringing lethargy, passive minds and dampening tongues

Irrespective of the position of the hands on the clocks,

Subtle beggars enter without a knock,

Looking askance at he,

The never-ending, suffocating *pulaar*,[16]

Cups of tea, coffee and then tea,

Mingled or unmingled, the onus is to maintain

The cycle of reciprocated visits,

Tangential conversations in sparse rooms,

In homes without cisterns,

Young children cavort in my house,

The peregrine Blond, ubiquitous but invisible,

Ambiguous and risible,

A flaxen halo of light above a black sea,

Except to the gabble of cheery children,

Spies for those who do not speak,

Small, smiling faces waving from the window,

Without preconceptions or prejudice,

We are living in two contiguous realities that never meet

A conspicuous duality that is hard to cheat

IX

Steaming Porridge and the day begins,

Amidst trains of breath chugging across icy rooms,

From mouth and kettle, in brittle air,

Inured to the cold of the Far North,

Where sledges are as long as a living room,

Bloodstained chariots seek the ice,

A *qamutik* as an heirloom,

Dogs with ampersand shaped tails

Skulk at the shoreline, beneath the moon

Living in the Arctic at an important time,

Our world is melting, but we are blind,

They call him Stiffi,

kinatin, kinatin?[17]

The Cambridge *embonpoint* was lost some time ago,

Hunaa, hunaa,[18]

And he garners a reputation in a cold place,

Where he must induce those to action,

Abstraction and reaction,

To tarry is to gain nothing

To delay is to lose something

Early December and finally out on the ice,

The soporific sound of smooth runners

Sliding across the frozen sea,

Months of fettered anguish at last set free,

And Qaanaaq, an army of receding fireflies,

Slippery slopes and muffled cries,

Tangential whip

And fan of dogs respond to hunter's call,

Thick pelts with small welts,

Harru, harru, atsuk, atsuk,[19]

Tangled traces and angry snarls,

Hak-hak, hak-hak,[20]

Defecating on the run, an unenviable task,

Fighting, wrestling, scattered faeces,

We navigate through a maze of frozen chess pieces,

That are checkmate until next summer

That wait for the endgame and the Grandmaster

X

They lay him to rest in a shallow December grave,

Spades break the mourners' silence and shovel the dirt in,

The occasional flint and raspings of metal,

Discordant, grating sound, harsh and dissonant,

No gravediggers or hearse, just local conscripts,

Torchlight beams illuminate grief-stricken faces,

A couple of short prayers,

Office of the Dead, the occasional placebo,

Simple and canonical,

And a winter dirge marks another premature coda,

Lived out in an ill-equipped hospital

Christmas Eve and the gospel of St John in a cosy,

Advent red, candle lit, window-frosted room,

Read out over the Advent Crown, beneath a hidden moon,

A Christmas saunter engenders gossip,

Thin ice and the *nanoq* skirts the settlement,[21]

Closer and closer they come,

A testament to changing times,

Some think the gun-less Englishman knows not the risks or the crimes,

The Arctic eco-icon wanders near,

Shadowy figures stumble in fear

The New Year is blown in from the East,
An assault on sore heads and fuddled minds,
His hut shudders and shakes, trembles and quakes,
A make-shift gate torn to pieces and fed to the wind,
The dogs fall silent amidst the chaos,
A few souls under siege, huddle and cower,
Coats pulled over heads as if sitting on sleds,
Dashing to nearby shelter, an awkward testudo,
With those unsteady at the back breaking rank.
Inside, evenings are late with Dr Zhivago,
Waking up to the three-stringed balalaika
And other wintry adagios,
Aloud in my head; alone in my bed
Early January and a pomegranate red stratum sky,
A cosmic fire creeps above the horizon,
Baffling, blanketing atomic empyrean,
Twelfth Night and grotesque, masked children loiter,
Shoulder to shoulder,
The *mitaartut*, and some are in epiphanic disguise,[22]
Herr, wenn die stolzen Feinde schnauben,
Als sie nun den König gehört hatten,
Fireworks on the sea ice gong Christmas to an end
Closing a festive chapter amidst young, small friends

Guileful glances diminish after some months,

And now just a tepid scepticism,

But, I begin to awake from the eternal slumber,

And the indeterminate shadowlands,

The sun was always shining somewhere else,

And the cento of misjudgements,

And miserable jumble of mistakes,

I am left hankering after light,

When uncertainty skulks over the place,

In ungarnished living rooms full of blank expressions

A New Year and a recrudescence,

Capering off to speak to folk about this and that,

Disengaged faces puzzle the Western mind,

Which requires clarity, expression of some kind,

Jibbed at the threshold by lost faces,

These people never trespass upon my mind,

Automatons whose view is not to be known,

On tired afternoons resting on stubs of time

No sallow cheeks at inquorate meetings,
No excuses, no apologies, just empty chairs,
And misplaced, enigmatic stares,
And lingering frustration spreading from wall to wall,
Eyes that see straight through me,
Circumambulating on snowy tracks,
Months of no sun and my ashen white face
And now troubled skin and dirty blond hair

Indolence festers in lazy living rooms,
Where those expected elsewhere loll and languish,
Where raised eyebrows mean 'yes', a
Screwed up nose 'no' and a shrug of the
Shoulders 'maybe', I guess,
Empty workplaces, but no comment or cavil from ones' peers,
Confrontation would be bad, best say nothing,
Silence in a stony place is the apotheosis of expression,
The virtue of the Arctic hunter,
Waiting at breathing holes, sitting motionless
In thoughtless kayaks, with harpoon in hand,
This, the playground of the uncritical mind,
A hot-bed of cultural misunderstandings and frequent digression,
Conspiring against us both, me and them,
On tired evenings resting on stubs of time

XI

Last day of January and at last a raddled sky,

Finally, oh finally, there is a night and day,

No more jeremiads,

No chance of doing a Blighty now,

But I miss the rain, I miss the grass,

I miss the soft chime of the College Chapel bell,

The days will become more normal now

Teams of dun, anxious dogs with cambered backs

Are now stationed on the ice, ready for off,

The sun will be back soon and now the temperature drops,

The cold stings and bites,

Cilia glued on frozen afternoons

Only to melt over hot coffee in wordless rooms,

Missed appointments and forgotten futures

Juggling hot air between kitchen and living room,

Memories sit in lazy chairs before *fjernsyn*,

And linger in fetid porches

Which offer fugitive hospitality,

Imagine a place without clocks,

A place where day and night are the same,

Both blown away by a selfish wind,

Imagine a place without maps,

As boundless as your memory

Let me tell you about the winds,

The *nigeq* brings a platonic white carpet of snow,

Warmer temperatures, cancelled adventures,

Blowing in new paradigms from the East,

Ruffling the inky feathers of the Raven,

With tinctured skies hidden behind a blurred white nothingness,

And then the *avannaq*, a strong wind from Etah

And the *pavanngainnaq* which comes from the North,

Making the water flat, spilling forth,

And perhaps the *anilatsiaq*, blowing icebergs,

Hither and thither, thither and hither,

And the *koororranertoq* like a *föhn* by the river,

Mild and moderate, cool and delicate,

And the *kanannaq* bringing mist and fog

Until the *pikannaq*, waiting and waiting agog,

But the hunters fear the *pigguahoq*,

Hiding sterile promontories,

Recalculating the profit and loss,

Scuppering plans, silencing the Church banns

Pangs of consciousness lurking in pungent rooms,

Viridian ice cubes parked outside dysfunctional homes,

Muffled figures in a mid-February liminal light,

Shuffle in the penumbra, wobble asunder,

Its in-betweenness, neither one thing nor the other,

A twilight of imprecision and vagueness,

A gaunt landscape on a bleak afternoon

XII

The freedom and simplicity of such an Arctic life,
Ihumaninahorjamahunga, ihumainahorjamahunga,[23]
People marvel at somebody following their heart's desire,
Tangled paths of idealism in a tidy home,
A Denys Finch Hatton of the North,
Alone, but not lonely, thinking, back and forth,
Like a ball pushed from flipper to flipper
In a pin-ball machine on a crumbling pier,
Subsiding into a British post-vocation silence,
Amidst the nostalgia of salt-sprayed slot machines

The air quivers on this frozen morning,
Beneath a chaffless sky,
Raised voices who have not slept,
Echo in my head until a late hour,
Until a later hour

And as I struggle through the museums of my mind,
The empty cabinets of forgotten knowledge,
The abstract exhibits of lost languages,
The dusty drawers of dying dialects,
The decaying tenses and moods of unparsed verbs,
Words wandering down grammarless avenues,
Prefixes parked at the end of an uncertain street,
Forgotten idioms floundering at crossroads,
Proverbs dropped off at the end of lonely cul-de-sacs,
A jumble of memories and foreign words on scraps
Of paper, parchment and purple post-its,
And trade wordy dreams on unwrapped mornings,
Oh, the deceiving sunshine of late February,
And these memories lost in a windy place

Kiangnaai, kiangnaai[24]

An elusive uncauterised aubade is finally, finally mine,

Light, hope and thoughts of future days,

But paradoxically no warmth,

Farewell to unredeemable darkness,

Basking in the coldest days of the year,

Thirty-five below, or somewhere near,

Light is now warmer than heat,

A low sun and long shadows,

Energy long lain fallow,

Is now awake, awake, awake

Arrested by rebukers who only surface on Friday nights,

Harshness in the Arctic comes in many forms,

But now, there is morning and evening,

And hazy, wobbly forms are once again the familiar

Lucid landscape borders,

No longer pale with grief,

And new tumid horizons

That are bolder than before,

Timid, no more

Tell me, what it is you see now the three month

Night is broken, now the light through

Yonder window breaks

XIII

Here, he stands, an idealist in a cold climate,

Amidst a reality of *ennui*, vacuous ambitions,

Breaches of disaffection and false conditions,

The Inugguit like to remind me,

We are born, we struggle and then we die.

Memento mori. Is that all? he may sigh

Should we just cling to Pascal's wager?

Wouldn't that be safer?

Communing with Nature, an infinite journey lies before me,

The lure of emptiness brings me here,

How emptiness and quests make good bed-fellows,

Elysian fields of sea ice lie ahead,

An unblemished, perfect expanse without end,

This naked landscape and

A mind aswarm with floating ideas and ambitions,

But has a finite, patchwork quilted landscape

Beckoned me to the Boundless?

Threatened me with a poisoned chalice?

This solitary enterprise,

This sequestered exercise,

Polar charioteers rule the frozen sea,

But an uncertain future beetles over thee

And now, the sun returns unimaginably fast,

Hours flit away in never-ending blue skies,

Spectacular sunsets mark the shank of the evening,

And the taxing courtship in a far away land,

Whose complex narrative now lies silently in the snow and sand,

Like one of those epic films that we love so much,

We almost made it, *mein Liebling*,

It was always just over the brow of a hill,

Just over the brow of a hill

We are all but experiential patches of films, books,

Photographs, friends and family sown together,

An album of expressions and looks,

A discography of distant, impersonated voices

That plays in our minds when moments are alone,

That dances in our loaned imagination.

A quilt of stitched and tailored composite identities whose whole

Is the sum of the parts and a little bit more

The far away scepter is a friendly face, perhaps

The kindest colonial master you will find,

Whose sovereignty is beginning to wane,

Is there something rotten in the state of Denmark?

Heaven will direct it,

But now, the sun and breeze burnish the ice,

And curled-up dogs lie in large circles on the pressure ridges,

Their rusty chains leading from a spike

Frozen into the ice like spokes on an old, buckled wheel,

Jaundiced patches of urine and dog faeces decorate the ice,

Tampering with its aesthetic of purity

Here I am, beached in a cold place,

Engulfed in a foreign culture,

Where the traditions ebb away,

Writhing like a Halibut on the ice,

Cooped up in an icy house,

Steeled to understand a strange idiom

And piece together the remains of animism

XIV

Haviggivik, a few half-deserted crumbs on a

Vast perfect white, Irish linen table cloth,

Starched and perfect,

Without the slightest knot or slub,

The hallmark of a well-appointed household,

Its appeal is immediate and unforgettable,

Discrete and untranslatable,

All have come to greet the thudding red machine,

Which arrives with such ado,

The post is eagerly unloaded onto a sledge

And the gathering disperses, traverses

Here, a tiny community clings on in a remote place

Living the slowest, most simple life imaginable

Where unfurled flags flap in the wind on Sunday afternoons,

Where *hila* determines the rhythm of life

And that is all.

A spyhole onto a pantheistic vision of man in unity with nature,

Remnants of an animistic worldview,

Shared amongst the select few,

Life stripped to its basics: subsistence, family

And lots of goodwill that slowly accrues,

On white winter days,

This is the cold heaven I came looking for

Contented couples live in cramped cabins,

Gaping and japing,

No women left for the many unspliced

For whom hunting comes first.

The *angatsuduk* lives alone[25]

With the radio on, an icon

And a few, dog-eared family snaps,

The *assak* live amongst well-fed dogs[26]

With cheery, round faces in hospitable homes,

Whose smiley children are magnetized to the stranger,

Following him around and around

Every Sunday the wind threatens to blow the place off the map,

The sky twists into a rictus of anguish,

Vulnerable lives sit in shaking houses,

Legs apart, behind smeared spyglasses,

Waiting for the *anuri* to unhinge the door,[27]

To an uncertain, undetermined future,

Empty huts smashed to pieces by unforgiving storms,

Their entrances lost behind walls of snow,

Oil heater in one corner, a bucket in the other,

A bed, television, crucifix, an aerial photograph perhaps,

And that is all

A brief encounter of jerry cans on packed snow,

Sighs, grins and a few words are traded,

Heavy lidded eyes spot a hunter from afar,

It is Illenguaq, *iih*, *iih* and[28]

A *taima* gongs the conversation to an end[29]

Discretion and subtlety are strangers' notions,
Scarred faces and deformities are exhibits for the visitor,
Lords of jealousy reign over spoiled futures,
The door is always open, no need to knock,
Raised eyebrows replace words and signal welcome,
Their wives are busy in the kitchen,
Tacenda is on the agenda in the living room,
Piles of shoes, *kamikker* and boots parley in the porch,[30]
Amidst skins, bloody pots and pungent pans,
The chads of a forgotten existence,
No hunting trophies on the wall
Icons for the foreign fool,
Dead seals on the kitchen floor
Are lunch, dinner and supper,
And not fodder for the taxidermist.
Adjacent to their quarry,
Men smoke pipes, sitting with lost expressions
And unconcealed flatulence in otherwise mute houses,
Next to diagrams, drinking black coffee,
One after the other

On the settee with a long *qamutik* as a foot-stool
Sits a bored girl playing a violent computer game,
Mission accomplished – all dead or lame,
Peace and violence juxtaposed in two realities
In the same room
Make for a strange, strange bride and bridge-groom

In the evening, the sky is bleached white,

Land and sky are the same,

Thronged in nothingness, whiteness everywhere,

The lack of distinction leaves me perplexed,

My thoughts retroflexed

And no longer sure-footed.

The grey, tatty A-framed houses with sealed up windows

And ladders on their roofs

Are beacons to carry me home.

Silence. Nothing. But then,

The contagious howls of the dogs

Echoing around the settlement,

Around and around

The wind draws contorted pictures in the ice,

Crooked smiles and bent expressions,

Broken circles and miniature mountain ranges,

Frozen castles with wonky towers

Are a playground for stumbling toddlers,

And behind, white crosses lost

Under a carpet of deep snow,

Like fallen soldiers without buglers or *caisson*,

But hidden names and spirits live on

In pseudo-reincarnation, in isolation

Where elderly men address children as 'grandfather'

And purloined names people the place

XV

Imagine a place without cars,

Trees, rain, thunder or grass,

A place where lost thoughts are awoken

By the smell of pungent *kiviat*,[31]

And a family of four feasting on

Long dead, fermented Little Auks,

Sitting on kitchen floors with open doors,

Legs at 120 degrees,

Like hungry scissors,

Sleeves rolled up,

Biting into the red flesh,

Smiling and grinning, smiling and grinning

A pell-mell in the middle of the night,

And to the site, of the fallen warrior of the ice,

The eco-icon of the North, shot dead,

Just below the head,

Outside, the second winter storm of the week is raging,

Inside, Sibelius plays to quivering curtains

And twisted walls that speak,

Lost in a swirl of amaranthine confusion,

The howling *nigeq* reverberates down the chimney,[32]

Scudding from East to West,

Finding every chink in the skirting board,

Every cranny and cleft in the ceiling,

Awakening us from our *langsam*, *schleppend* existence

Kiatak, and a journey to the end of the world,[33]

Through a silent white wilderness,

Beneath the halos of the sun,

Across the frigid air of the evening shadow,

Anaesthetised on the sledge,

Numb and obtund, on the way

To a borderless place,

Away from the world of objects

And towards the universe of sounds,

Where words are noise and not scribbles,

Where the raw beauty and inhospitableness

Of the Arctic share the same bed, the same quibbles

Harking back to a prelapsarian unity,

Remote for me, but not for them,

Why do our words for 'remoteness'

Carry such negative connotations?

Such sinister associations.

Rubble fields to my left, pyramids to my right,

Transmogrifying ice all around,

The dogs' howls echo and echo

Around and around,

Ringing empty the sound of wilderness,

Marking their territory on a corner of Northumberland Island,

The memory of the echo lives on,

Circling in my mind like an ontological merry-go-round,

Taking me back to places I have been,

To the cities that I have seen,

To the dreams that I dream,

Stories and narratives speak in an abandoned settlement,

Small cabins ripped to pieces by the wind,

But memories sit on empty shelves in Qeqertarhhuaq

A spring tide and the squeaking, chittering

Brash ice of April, repining

Under a lavender, empyreal sky

As the moon reaches her perigee

In these days of sempiternal Arctic light,

The ice creaks like a rusty door beneath my feet,

The new sea ice is thin and

The tusks and wrinkled skin

Have gone, beyond and beyond.

The midnight sun peers through the window

At the consciousness dozing

On the hard wooden sleeping platform,

Juggling taxonomies in my mind

Pushing certain ontologies aside

To the drip of the thawing walrus

Outside, there is stillness, just stillness

Inside, there is silence, just silence,

This is the lost life of uncorrupted morals

That civil society eschewed,

Whose members traded freedom for

The lie of material happiness,

Imprisoned reality and canned food

The pumping of the brass Primus paraffin pressure stove

In the middle of the lit night,

Here, there is life too,

Delicate, oval footprints tip-toe across the snow,

The Arctic Fox manages to survive, somehow,

The Raven must have the intelligence to go elsewhere,

But apparently there are plenty here

XVI

I happened upon
An immaculate white wilderness,
Timeless and silent,
In a never-ending winter.
And there sits Hiorapaluk
In the stillness of an Arctic sunlit night.
The sea ice hides a world underneath,
And the future for this community,
Untainted shadows spread across the fjord
Like water spilt on a white carpet,
Frozen, stiff hair in the cool month of May

Fjords and *kangerduks* are empty places,[34]
Whose deep waters are unknown,
Hidden beneath the pure and austere,
White unfenced pathway across the sea,
And the mythical landscape before me
Where solitude speaks its name,
Where 'ownership' for once is not such a meaningful word
As recent perambulations and hesitations disappear
Under the new, thick May snow,
Can the uncrowded vista whiten any more?
Why is the never-ending whiteness so alluring?
Its simplicity, whiteness and perfection draws
Me deeper into the wilderness,
Taking my mind elsewhere to an other,
Lost, forgotten world
Beyond the radio fuzz that blows into the kitchen and to
Where the chaffs of the day are unprolific,
Sighing and groaning like the ice under my feet

Hiorapaluk – lost digits and private existences,
And the flies that seem to come back from the dead,
The filth and chaos of the smoky bachelor's cabin,
Water on the Primus and the cat's cradle in our hands,
Angatsuduk and *arnaduk* are[35]
An anomaly in a small, coupled place
Where the hunter always leaves his trace

On the 5th of May, a coalition of sea birds
Sits on the sea ice in grey and white plumage,
Congregating and making plans,
Looking cold, lost and ill-at-ease,
Calligraphic rivers wind through the ice,
Icy ascenders going above the waistline,
Beneath a sky without contrails or vapour trails

Womens' faces that show no emotion whatsoever
But subscribe to a symbiotic relationship with nature,
Here, an antidote to modern civilisation,
At times and in parts, at least,
Oh, the pith and gist of the endless sun,
The nightless days and the children's fun
And the long soughs coming from huts
That whisper a pot-pourri of similar subjects
About this and that

XVII

The Far North – a harsh Romanticism,

Lashings of time and space to think, cogitate, ponder,

Reflect upon and think again,

I lie amongst the herbage of June,

During the husks of the day,

With imbalanced Circadian rhythm,

Under a diaphanous light,

A head full of aphorisms in this introspective place,

Drowned in my infinitely circular thoughts

About my life, about our rented existence,

About the pith of the matter,

And the fundamental *Ur*-way of being,

Thoughts that lead nowhere,

But to the beginning, the beginning

It is summer in Qaanaaq,

The dogs sit with their stigmata

Under the implacable glare of the sun

That dazzles and circles above our heads,

Without pausing to think or sink,

The sea ice is broken, shattered and scattered,

Like a love story with a bad end,

Rodin like sculptures of ice stand-off on the beach,

Hewed by *hila*,

Le Penseur, La Danaïde, Le Baiser et La Misère,

Silted shoes of summer,

Arctic Poppies, Rhododendrons, bilberries and lichen

That gild the lilly and

Are neighbours on the summer bog

A thought, even a possibility, can shatter and transform us,

Some spare a moment for the furniture of the Universe,

My thoughts turn to those living in choked cities

That we call 'civilised',

To the stain of industry that

Might yet stipple and dapple this white heaven

Of this Green Land,

Living without industry is surely an ideal,

Swerving 'progress' and 'development'

And thus living without fumes and noisy *spiel*

And to the meaningless of

Self-imposed destruction,

To the prisoners of monotony

Whose bilked lives are lived in grey offices

And expressionless trains

That rattle and rumble

Late into the night,

Chidden by their superiors,

But pursuing careers which will make their mothers proud

On the edge of a bleak future,

Of water-stricken mega cities and

A mixed-up, globalised world,

The megaphone of universal hip-hop

Blaring to the masses in corrupt English,

Give me The Rolling Stones, Shostakovich and Rach.,

Give me words that stimulate a cabaret of expressions

When thoughts of previous lovers are lost to the wind,

The poet seeks the purity of the tribe,

The nomads of a disappearing age

Who dog-sledged in the blurred tedium of the polar desert,

But the vision has long gone,

The last drop of romance has dissolved in the evening sun

And to the debted youth of England

Spilling over an *overfullt* island

With their balding heads

And lazy, ugly demotic,

Living busy, muddled lives,

Toasting the celebration of idiocracy

And the loss of standards and decency

And the absurdity of post-modernist Britain,

On display, in television and magazine.

And the whole plurality of humanity.

And vulgar America,

Strange conservatism and how much you 'make'

Put elocution on the curriculum,

And thus spare the tympanum

Before Estuary English makes a mess of us all

Thinning candleflames flicker and whisper,

On evenings that are self-doubting,

Amidst all the *thèmes du jour*

That are not discussed,

The changing *Landsgesicht*,

And the silence of my political coevals,

And the loss of iconicity,

The Brussels bureaucrats

Who build a new empire

Without the mandate of the people,

The never-ending rain that

Sings a morning madrigal

Running down the gutters of steep streets,

And the puddled pavements glazed

In the light of nostalgic, bow-fronted shop windows,

Now that my upholstered thoughts turn to home

XVIII

And now time to leave my *Elsewhere*,

Time to return to my *Lebenswelt*

Of chloroform, neutered thought,

And poppycocks political correctness,

To the hullabaloo of the circus,

To a different kind of *Mitsein*,

To the hubbub, hurry-scurry and helter-skelter

Of the minutiae of modern life,

Of the millions and billions,

To cramped, urban sprawl-sopped England,

Whose open hands embrace and solace

The spittled zoo of globalisation,

Packed in their tiny, terraced houses,

Many-hued faces, faiths and fancies

Upon England's lost mountain's green,

Sitting in their identical motorcars,

With idle expressions and bad postures,

And a roster of dilemmas,

Waiting for scuttled hopes and scotched futures

To close clotted narratives

That prowl in din-dinted parlours

Notes

1. 'A buoy made out of a seal bladder, tied to the kayak and placed behind the hunter'
2. *kadluna* is the Inuit term for the white European or North American
3. 'perhaps, maybe'
4. A traditional greeting
5. 'God'
6. 'dogs'
7. 'in the old days'
8. *taffi* 'the local drinking den'; – *mut* is the allative case ending, suggesting movement towards the drinking den
9. 'sledges'
10. The planet 'Venus'
11. Inuit deity and term for climate, weather, consciousness and mind
12. 'shaman'
13. A mythical representation of somebody who has been rejected from Inuit society and who escapes to the wilderness
14. 'war'
15. 'sea ice'
16. The Inuit practice of visiting one another
17. 'Who are you?'
18. An expression of surprise
19. Inuit dog-sledging calls: 'left, right'
20. A dog call meaning 'get going'
21. 'polar bear'
22. Polar Eskimo tradition of dressing up in disguise on Twelfth Night
23. 'I want my mind to be open to thoughts'
24. A traditional phrase used when the sun came back on the 19th of February

25 'bachelor'

26 'A diligent, hard working hunter'

27 'wind'

28 The Polar Eskimo word for 'yes'

29 The word for 'enough'

30 'Traditional seal skin boots'

31 'Fermented Little Auks'

32 'A wind from the East that blows most strongly in February and March'

33 Local name for Northumberland Island

34 Polar Eskimo word for 'fjord', literally 'empty place'

35 'bachelors' and 'spinsters'

Lightning Source UK Ltd.
Milton Keynes UK
UKOW03f0626071014

239719UK00001B/77/P

9 781909 300620